Psychological Tricks of The Enemy

Resurrecting The Dead

By

Ismael Muwakkil Muhammad

Copyright 2022 © Ismael Muwakkil Muhammad

ISBN 979-8-88589-545-3

Table of Contents

Chapter One.. 11

Chapter Two 24

Chapter Three.. 33

Chapter Four 43

Chapter Five 52

You must be considerate of yourself when you sit down and dine at the table of a ruler; and not be prone to a voracious appetite, for the meat is deceptive, the wine is a mocker, and the strong drink is raging, and whosoever that has been deceived thereby is not wise.

Every program has at least two purposes in life: the one for which it is written and the other for which it was not.

He who reforms himself has done more toward reforming the public than a noisy crowd of impotent scholars.

When a man lights a candle, He does not seek or attempt to hide its Light; He places it in a candlestick and lets it shine upon all within.

FORWARD

Know all men by these presents **THAT I AM** Greetings of Salutation by Visitation, in the presentation of this modest little Book, as is entitled "Tricknology of the Enemy: Psychological Warfare." I Am elated for you to know that I Am a student of the teachings of the Most Honorable Elijah Muhammad and under the banner of the Honorable Minister Louis Farrakhan. I have taken the time and energy to express and to convey My sentiments of what I have perceived from these life-giving teachings, and also to relate how these teachings have helped Me and how they have raised Me to a perpendicular square and out of a mental state of darkness into the Divine Light of the Creator. The teachings of the Most Honorable Elijah Muhammad have raised Me to a heightened level of Conscious Enlightenment that no method of the conventional system established by society could ever have accomplished. It is a fact that the teachings of the Most Honorable Elijah Muhammad are right and exact and that they have the propensity to transform lives. So, it is extremely an honor to give Honor and Salutation to the above two Great Lights, and the third, the Honorable Minister Jabril Muhammad. He supplied Me with his precious time and infinite wisdom.

So, this modest little Book is based upon My constant and diligent research and study and derived from My personal experience(s), My association(s) with others and their experience(s), and of My observation of others in their experience(s). At some time in our life, many of us have asked ourselves some very profound questions regarding our physical existence, such as who am I? What is the purpose of my existence in this physical and materialistic world in which we reside? Am I born just to live for a short period and then die? We have posted just a few queries to understand the purpose of life's hidden meaning and where we fit into the scheme of things.

There are many things that I wish to convey to you, and I find it most difficult at times to adequately express in certain terms, since seeing that you are not and have not been paying any attention to the operations being conducted in the daily activities of your surroundings. For when you, yourselves, should be teachers of the knowledge, I have found that you are in need again to receive the teachings of the Oracles of the Creator. You, the masses of the [people are being destroyed because of your lack of knowledge.

Be ye not as the horse or the mule who does not have knowledge or an understanding. For now, there has come unto you one that grieves for your constitution, that you should not perish. There is a similitude for those who were charged with the Mosaic Law, but who have subsequently failed in their obligations entrusted to them, regarding the knowledge conveyed to them to impart to you is that of a donkey who carries a multitude of books that they do not understand seeking to be teachers of the Oracles of the Creator. Evil is the similitude of those who have falsified the signs of the Creator and is thus guiding the masses of the people to do what is wrong due to their ignorance.

So, now we must rebuild the house: a destroyed house based upon our ignorance. And for a house to be great again, it must be furnished and decorated with all manner of precious gems and vessels; but you must know that just vessels of gold and silver are not the only objects found within a great house, but also are found vessels made of earth and that which is made of wood as well. Just as some houses and vessels are good to honor, some houses and vessels are bad and dishonored. Therefore, if a man conforms and purges himself, he shall become a vessel raised in honor, sanctified and purified through the fire, and meet for the Master`s use.

Wherefore, in the Theos of all things that are to be created, it must first be thought of and thus visualized by the mind`s eye and then formulate a nisus into what this creation is to appear on the surface after the process is completed and then crystalize it into a reality.

Hear My voice, oh ye people, for you must break this vicious cycle of psychological mind manipulation. Tell Me, with whom have I taken counsel? And from whence have I received instruction? And who has taught and continues to teach Me the knowledge and shows Me the Way to understanding that leads Me in the Path of just judgment and righteousness? Answer Me if you know.

My sincere and divine hope that you encompass and enjoy the richness of the flavor and texture of this most gratifying and nutritional meal that I have taken the time and pleasure to most out of love for you and have prepared for your edification. And when you back away from the table, after sating your hunger, that while you are digesting your meal, that you give serious contemplation and reflection upon this meal's life-giving source and strive from this day forward to the cleansing of your mind and body and thus restoring them into good health and prosperity. All of you will act according to their disposition, but the Creator knows best who it is guided on the right way. For surely, never will the Creator change the condition of a people until they change it themselves.

Thank you in advance for your time, patience, and consideration in having the courage to make an effort and pick up this modest little Book of Mine and consume its contents. I sincerely hope you will revise and receive the benefits of the knowledge contained herein and utilize it to the best of your ability. Mind you, as I do not expect you to accept the contents herein on face value, because I expect you to investigate and make a proper and thorough examination and determination for yourself, to deduce if I have presented My Self to you in righteous dealings. Know that the Creator grants His wisdom to whom He pleases, and to whom His wisdom is granted has received indeed a great benefit overflowing, but none can or will be able to grasp the message conveyed but men of understanding. It is all about Supreme Mathematics! Travel safely! It has truly been a blessing to have known you

Peace, Peace!

Ismael Muwakkil Muhammad

Chapter One

Society

We live in a world governed by a small group of people whose interests are not yours, as their primary function is desired. Their expressed intent is to maintain psychological oppression over you by attacking the sensory perception of your thought process through mind manipulation and under a banner and a false sense of illusion that is termed society. You may ask, what is Society? One could only imagine, think, feel and believe that society would be the whole masses of the people coming together in unity and for the common good of everybody involved. And it is on this point; I express such a gross and false misconception.

Upon a closer examination of this term, society as a whole group of people comes together in unity for the common good of all the parties contained within this group. As conveyed, this term group is expressing bias and partiality to only a very small assemblage; it specifies and distinguishes itself apart from the whole. It has, in fact, deliberately and blatantly omitted and excluded you… the masses of the people from this equation. For society, as it stands and functions as nothing other than a psychological thief of oppression. And you have been duped into a false sense of security because of your inability to want to rule over and govern your affairs and selves: meaning taking responsibility for your action(s). So, you have now given yourselves over to the thieves.

"The trees went forth on time to anoint a king over them, and they said unto the olive tree, Reign thou over us. But the olive tree said unto them, Should I leave my fatness, wherewith by me they honor God and man, and go to be promoted over the trees? And the trees said unto the fig tree, Come thou and reign over us. But the fig said unto them, Should I forsake my sweetness, and my good fruit, and go to be promoted over the trees? Then said the trees unto the vine, Come thou and reign over us. And the vine said unto them, Should I leave my wine, which cheereth God and man, and be promoted over the trees? Then said all the trees unto the bramble, Come thou, and reign over us. And the bramble said unto the trees, If in truth ye anoint me king over you, then come and put your trust in my shadow". Judges 9:8-15

Society, as it stands, has placed upon you iron-clad rules and regulations, ordinances, statutes, policy statements, directives, and specified registrations designed to manipulate you into the relinquishment of all of your Inalienable, Natural, and Vested Rights, and those of your descendants as well, that you are endowed with at birth to possess, as so illustrated below:

"And Esau said to Jacob, Feed me, I pray thee, with that same red pottage; for I am faint, his name was Edom. And Jacob said, Sell me this day thy birthright. And Esau said, Behold, I am at the point to die: and what profit shall this birthright make to me? And Jacob said, Swear to me this day, and he swore unto him: and he sold his birthright unto Jacob. Then Jacob gave Esau bread and pottage of lentils;

he ate and drank, arose, and went his way; thus, Esau despised his birthright". Gen. 25:30-34

And through the tricknology of the enemy, you have unwittingly abrogated and regulated these rights to others to usurp them as they choose. You have thus subjected yourself to the level of what is termed a Loose Fish. When before this relinquishment, you were hailed as a Fast Fish. And by relinquishing and thus regulating yourself to society's standards and way of life, you have now, in fact, been re-captured, and thus have been transformed into what society has now termed and classified you as its Fast Fish!

You are scratching your heads and asking yourselves, what is a Loose Fish and a Fast Fish? Answer: A Loose Fish, upon examination and reflection, is considered and now classified as that… whatever it may be, which is fair game for the taking; and further upon this line of reflection, a Fast Fish is something that belongs to and is in actual possession of the party in question: whether this collateral is tangible or intangible, it is technically fast when it is in the possession – by any medium at all controllable, when it bears a seal, mark, or any other recognized symbol of ownership by the individual possessor.

Let us examine and obtain a closer analysis. Here is a very profound and illustrative story of a classic example, depicting faith to the message I wish to convey. So please pay very close attention. It starts as a dispute between two gentlemen over a particular piece of property. A gentleman had an issue concerning a certain piece of property in his possession. So, he consulted with a friend about what sort of action he should do, and his friend advised him to seek counsel to represent him. So, he sought counsel and hired a very distinguished counselor for his defense by the name of Mr. Erskine. The acting and presiding judge over the matter was the Honorable Lord Ellenborough.

The argument for the defense was that the property was in the rightful possession of the defendant. And in the course of his defense, the witty Mr. Erskine commenced with the illustration of the defenses' position by alluding to a previous situation and a similar case involving a criminal conversation, wherein a gentleman, after, in a vain effort of trying to circumvent his wife`s promiscuousness, at long last abandoned her upon the sea of life. And during the span of a course of years, the gentleman relented and wanted her back. And then he learned that she had someone else, so he proceeded to institute a cause of action in a court of law to recover her as his possession again.

Mr. Erskine then continued to craft his position and stated that he held her fast, although the gentleman had originally harpooned the lady. If not for the great stress caused upon him by her brusque promiscuousness, he ultimately had abandoned her, thereby making her a Loose Fish, enabling another gentleman to subsequently re – harpoon her… and therefore making her and everything associated with her his property. And here, Mr. Erskine rested his case for the defense. And upon the judge`s examination of all the evidence presented and the testimony provided by the plaintiff and the defendant ruled in favor of the defense.

Now, I contend that the lady and how society has regulated itself as the possessor of a particular piece of property as collateral are reciprocally illustrative of each other.

Is it not in the saying coming from the masses of the people's mouth that possession of a property is only half of the law regarding how one came to possess the property. Possession, however. You look at it as the "whole of the law"! What do you think are the bodies and the souls of the serfs, peasants, slaves, and peons and all that is within them, who have relinquished their rights and given them to another but a Fast Fish… of which possession is the whole of the law, period!

If the doctrine of the Fast Fish is generally applicable in today's society, and we know this to be a fact; therefore, the doctrine of the Loose Fish, with all intent and purpose, is internationally and universally known is applicable as well. Man's Rights and Liberties; men's mind(s) and their opinion(s); the principles of their religious beliefs and philosophies derived from them are nothing short of being a Fast

Fish, and upon your relinquishment of these rights ultimately becomes a Loose Fish.

Let us consider the perpetual turbulence in society`s social fabric, and its manifestation in another story, the story of Joseph. Where Joseph dreamed a dream, in which he then narrated it to his brothers, and he says to them, for behold, we were binding sheaves in the field, and lo, my sheaf arose and stood upright; and behold your sheaves stood round about and made obeisance to my sheaf. And his brothers became unsettled and asked him, shalt thou indeed reign over us? Or shalt thou indeed have dominion over us? His brothers began to harbor hatred and resentment for Joseph for the statement that he had made.

Subsequently, Joseph had dreamed yet another dream, in which he again expounded upon this dream to his brothers and his father. He said to them, I have dreamed a dream more; and behold, the sun and the moon, and the eleven planets made obeisance to me. His father was astonished by such a dream and asked Joseph, what is this dream that thou hast dreamed?

Shall I and thy mother and brothers come to bow ourselves to thee to the earth? But his brothers hated Joseph all the more and sought to devise a plan to rid themselves of Joseph once and for all, and they were all in one accord, so they schemed a plan and got rid of Joseph.

Now let us examine Joseph's story here and give it just a measure. First, we can assert with some measure of assurance that the ten brothers are being depicted here to us as operating as one collective human social group, with all of their arrogance based upon their physical strength and massive size in numbers, and also with contempt of the older and wiser experience as well. Secondly, we can also deduce another aspect from this story. Because, what I can also perceive that is being depicted here to us, is how the better or righteous half of human nature sometimes has to struggle to assert itself against the baser and the unrefined standards of a mass mentality. The better or righteous half in nature of the individual will always have to struggle hard against the negative collective standards. The unregenerate human nature seems to be the last hurdle to cross in morality until it learns to harmonize and unite the two forces.

Whereas Joseph`s subsequent slavery and his placement in prison are the types of conditions that a righteous Man must suffer through and also endure the foibles and obliquity of others, so that he may, one day by chance bring about a change of good in others, and that he may also bring about and develop within his nature a character, and the manifestation of the Light of the Divine Creator within himself. Without suffering, sorrow, struggling and striving – a spiritual war within oneself, you will not be capable of attaining your full potential, strength, and stature. Because with every difficulty, there comes to ease! Through these harsh lessons of ours, we must come to learn the true essence of what good and sound morals and values are.

Wherefore, the slave must work, and he must la-bor, and this work and labor are not for himself, but others as an act of charity, so that he may learn and grow in knowledge. And suppose he performs this task in the right frame of mind. In that case, he will ultimately understand and expose the shallow and hollowness of society's idleness, the ridiculous position of their arrogance, and the frailty of their power, which permits acts of injustice to occur unchecked. And the prisoner, who, thus being innocent of any criminal offense, is placed into a prison typesetting, must not maintain a befogged mind – hatred of his situation. Still, he must take into account and consideration his position and how it came to be, and take the time to study and educate himself and then reflect, and increase his spiritual understanding, liberties and opportunities and perhaps then apply his wisdom to show by contrast the darker and most impenetrable the prison in whose grip resides his unjust incarcerators. The ultimate test is whether the innocent Man, who has been placed in prison and is being subjected to cruel and harsh conditions, can remain firm in his resolve.

Society is a standardized network system created and designed to lead and herd you like sheep, and like cattle, for sheep and cattle are tamed and domesticated creatures of the field, in a direction that is not in your best interest, for the systematic self – destruction of your structural and mental capacity to think and or operate independently for yourselves. Society says, I will mislead them, and I will create false desires; I will order them to slit the ears of cattle and deface the nature created by the Creator.

In society`s efforts to maintain its stranglehold and control upon you, the masses, it devised a judicial system, termed an institution of law to enforce its authority and possession of you as a people; and as a detriment to further solidify your contract with them over you. One has only to look toward this judicial system, which, as it is society`s most trusted institution and primary source of operation and income; and its function is solidifying the contractual agreements between them and you, and their only concern is with the generation of vast sums of revenue as it is a catalyst of their prison system. And if you bear witness to this fact, that the vast majority of the people, has at one point and time… including relatives, friends, and associates in their life have had an encounter with what is termed the police. And this same vast majority has at least been arrested, convicted, and have either received fines, probation, jail time, or prison time – for one matter or another or in any different combinations or all of the above. This system is not concerned with justice as you can see that its concern is only securing a conviction, for only in a conviction, by whatever method can revenue be generated – pass through.

You are being tricked and deceived by those who do not have your best interest. So, what are you going to do? Are you just going to continue sitting and being tricked and deceived? Or are you going to study and educate yourself, break the yoke from around your neck, and release the shackles from your feet to be liberated and free yourself from this mental state of bondage?

Chapter Two

Psychological Warfare

Many of you may query why I would entitle a portion of this modest little Book Psychological Warfare. There is any reason(s) for such a venture, but only one will suffice herein. So, what is psychological warfare? Answer: It is a systematic process in the acculturalization, manipulation, and psychological oppression of a people's minds. The subjugation of the thought process of a people placed in a hypnotic self–destructive fashion, and the divorcement of man from himself. The intoxicating inducement of a dependent indoctrination of security that arrests and incarcerates the mind is an even greater form of capture.

"For we wrestle not against flesh and blood, but principalities, against powers, against the rulers of the darkness of this world, against spiritual wickedness in high places." Eph. 6:12

This war against your mind did not just crop up overnight but is due to careful and elaborate plotting and planning and has been in operation for quite some time. It started with the miseducation of your forefathers, migrated on down to your parents, and has now ultimately stood at your threshold. You have only simplified the situation by your willing and unknowing indulges.

Houston, we have a problem! For you have regulated yourselves to the pollution of the manufactured toxic poison(s), giving strong drinks to those who are ready to perish, i. e., such as heroin, spice, k – 2, crack, cocaine, meth, pills, fentanyl, and religion are self – induced poisonous drugs designed to penetrate and impregnate the mind to the deterioration of the body.

You may say, how is/or can my religion be classified as a drug? Are you a religious hater? I will respond to your second query first. Answer: No, I Am Not a religious hater; I just do not believe in it as you think you do. For religion is not a song and dance, clapping and the stomping of feet, because none of this can and will gravitate you to the Divine Creator and get you into the kingdom of Heaven. As it was created and designed as a step–by–step ladder or phase to aid you in your mental and spiritual progression. You have yet to receive and experience spiritual enlightenment. Although you should be teachers of yourself eating strong meat, instead, you have only relapsed to the stature of a baby, again requiring milk, and the milk you are to the stature of a baby, again requiring milk. The milk you are receiving has and is dulling your mental and spiritual senses. When I was a child, I spoke and acted out My childish way. I thought like a child. Therefore My understanding was childish as well. But when I became a Man, I subsequently dissipated all of My childish activities.

Now, I will proceed to the first query for a response. Answer: Religion, as it is being expressed, is a highly sophisticated drug of the utmost magnitude geared to ensnare the minds of the masses using a doctrine that will have and make you think and act in a certain semi-automatic fashion; and anyone who does not think and act – believe as you believe are of the devil, in comport to as to how you were taught; as this doctrine defines and describes the nature and characteristics of this devil. You being intoxicated with this very special and different religious belief and philosophy, you have become assiduous and amnestic, to where you are now functioning in the capacity of this devil. To where you will maim and kill anyone outside of your respective doctrine(s) – so-called religion (drug). Activities for which you have performed in the name of religion: Accord, all of the religious wars fought by your so-called zealots and fanatics of these religions. Your respective religions have been compromised and infiltrated by individuals unknown to you. Your well(s) – doctrine(s) have been contaminated with a synthetic toxic poison, designed to erode your most valued institution – your common sense.

For in My travels with those I have associated with, and My observations of the users of drugs in whatever form they chose to indulge in have lied, cheated, stole, betrayed, abandoned, maimed, and killed one another all in the name of, and for the sake of their respective drug(s) of choice.

These drug(s) have you so infatuated with them that nothing else seems to exist outside them. They have you so intoxicated that everything in your original teachings, which has instructed you to refrain from doing and acting out evil, you perform them with relish. Then you make such childish and lame excuses as to why you have performed some of the refrained activities, and you legitimize your reason(s) as to why you perform them and the others as acts of doing the will of your God. You are so sadly deluded! You are the eighty–five percent... deaf, dumb, and blind: easily to be led in the wrong direction and hard to lead in the right direction. You must come to learn to know and comprehend your religious text, as they speak of such beings as these, as the dead have been commissioned to bury their dead! Examine this text for yourself, let us reason together, and then determine after your examination concludes how the physical dead can bury its physically dead unless, in its conveyance, it is describing the mentally dead.

This psychological oppression has you so trapped in a systematic web of mind manipulation and drained into a self-induced self–destruct mode. There will be population control! You must come to ++realize and know what this population control is. By your divorcement of yourself from yourself, and your subsequent remarriage to the manufacturer(s) of your drug(s), and your respective drug(s) of choice: you have therefore and therein relinquished all of your rights to your name and self to circumvent any type of relief or remedy, i. e., your body, name, exemplar, fingerprints, footprints, DNA, RNA, and your mind, to which is your personal property, to which now no longer belong to you, But it is now the property, as collateral in possession of someone else. Because of your lack of knowledge, you did not know that property is not a capitalistic invention. But that property is an instrument, a test of responsibility, and a test of Man`s character. That property is how dominion can be exercised. But, to sinful men, it means theft, the supposed right to expropriate from others.

Although you, the masses, are lost in the wilderness and possess a misapprehension about your deed(s) and your action(s) as being righteous: there has to be a way to bring you back into alignment with the Divine Creator. What method or approach may I convey to the masses that you will comprehend the sinful act(s) of your deed(s)? What method or approach may I convey to you, the misconception of the path you are traveling and how it leads you to the abyss, under the guise of being righteous, is only a pigmented illusion? What method or approach may I demonstrate to you, the unconscious masses, that the religion you belong to and the school(s) of thought you are affiliated with and receiving instructions only lead you to the abyss and death? It is without a doubt that you, the masses, do not perceive that your respective religious order(s) and leader(s) can perform no act(s) of evil, for they are convinced that, by the sermons alone of your respective leader(s), that they are just and good.

"Can the blind lead the blind? Shall they not both fall into the ditch?" Luke 6:39

Architect of the Universe: The Supreme Being, The Creator of this Material Universe. And He has endowed Me with the Supreme Knowledge, Supreme Understanding, and Supreme Wisdom, to combat evil against My Self from grand theft: and being one of the chosen; I have been commissioned to trace out the chosen that are lost in the wilderness and impart the knowledge of the Secret Mysteries of the Kingdom of Heaven. And I Am endowed with the ability to guard and combat My Self tenaciously against the "thieves of oppression.—the rulers of the darkness of this world. I implore of you that I may be bold in your presence, with that confidence where-with I think to be bold against some, who think that I walk according to the flesh; even though I walk in the flesh, I do not war after the flesh: as My weapons of warfare are not carnal, but mighty in the Divine Creator for pulling down strongholds and casting down imaginations in the high places. I Am commis-sioned, and it is only My duty to convey the message of the Creator to you, and it is up to you whether or not you are to reject it or accept it for what it is; for it is Divine Knowledge!

"Unto you, it is given to know the mystery of the kingdom of God; but unto them that are without, all these things are done in parables: that seeing they may see, and not perceive, and hearing they may hear, and not understand; lest at any time they should be converted, and their sins should have forgiven them." Mark 4:11-12

Chapter Three

Religion

When one thinks about religion, the first thing that comes to the forefront of the mind is the singing, the clapping, and the patting of the feet. Then from there, you would have the fire and brimstone sermon of the preacher, pastor, rabbi, Imam or minister, and thus proceed to the collection of the alms, then get into a little more singing, clapping, and the patting of the feet; and then finally followed by the disbursement. Throughout this routine ritual, the drama of your life unfolds, where the religious leaders are engaging in extramarital affairs with members of their respective congregations and even outside of their congregations as well, leaving their spouses starving; and the members likewise are engaged and having similar affairs with other members and with those who are non – members: whoremongering; gossiping; backbiting; slandering; fighting; and thievery. For this is what your religion has been designed and regulated to.

Whereas religion in its true form, for which it was created and designed, was to bring one back into the realm and conformity of the "All "pervading presence. In its creation, religion was originally designed as a step–by–step process or ladder to receive spiritual enlightenment. Religion derives from the Latin word "Religare," from re, again, and ligare, to bind and is meant to bind the soul to the Creator. But you have permitted and allowed yourself to be hoodwinked and deceived through the tricknology of the enemy, who has not only modified, altered, and amended your religion and its dictates but has changed it, for no one can truly attain Heaven or a state of Divine Felicity on what is being performed and practiced in the churches, mosque, temples, or synagogues of today, where the cable-tow to the Divine has been completely severed.

How has my religion been infiltrated, especially when I know what the Lord has taught me? Do you! Do you believe what you say to be true? I do not think you have the foggiest or slightest idea of what has happened and what is happening to you. You are following and practicing what you have been taught and led to believe and practice by society. And you can bear witness to the facts, as I have most succulently presented them to you. And I will answer your query, but first, you must know this as well.

If you were to examine the First International Communist Gathering, you would discover Karl Marx proclaiming that he was not a Marxist. And you will also find published in a magazine out of Paris containing the following words of endearment as expressed by Karl Marx, to wit:

"Using the triumphant worldly proletariat, we will create the Universal Soviet Socialist Republic with its capital in Jerusalem. In this way, we will take possession of the wealth of all nations. This is how the prophecies of our holy prophets of Talmud will be fulfilled".

Karl Marx was also the religious fanatic who instituted a most deadly weapon of mass destruction so destructive that it would reduce the minds of the masses and their respective religions to nothing. By the way, that weapon of mass destruction is called "jargon." For jargon is a jumble of words and phrases generally not understood by anyone outside their respective group; it is a provincial dialect and a language peculiar to a locality. It is mostly known as confused and unintelligible talk.

This jargon has been incorporated into your daily diet and activities, and way of life. It was first instituted and utilized by your great grandparents to your grand grandparents, and now by you, with such a devastating effect, that you now classify and define this jargon as pig Latin or slang, as a normal for your language expression and justification for your lack of knowledge. And you are and have been feeding this jargon to your young and are allowing your young to be fed this poisonous staple – jargon by others, yet you claim to love yourself and your young. Look at the mental state you have permitted yourselves and the lives of your children to fall; into a sickening state of evil, and you are slowly deteriorating.

And for your further improvement, you will find most interesting is one of the Protocols of the Elders of Zion, which expresses the following in domination over you as a people:

"When we come into our kingdom, it will be undesirable for us that there should exist any other religion… we must therefore sweep away all other forms of religion. It does not matter if, for our means, we have to fill the world with materialism and repugnant atheism since the day we become triumphant, we will universally preach the religion of Moses that, by its codified and thoroughly dialectical system, will bring all the peoples of the world into subjection to us'.

In the first stage of the penetration of the doctrine and the subsequent impregnation of the subliminal suggestion of this jargon, you acquired an asocial personality with strong delinquency trends, with an inadequate judgment of reality, and often confused and disorganized states of mind, and with a grossly immature and impulsive nature; and also compounded by the religious indoctrination of your brain, you were considered to be what was termed at that time as "Zombies', walking around aimlessly in a dazed catatonic state of existence, looking for a brain: the ability to think and operate independently, and anyone that you encountered who were not of a similar mentality as yourselves, you killed them and devoured their brains in an effort, and with the hopes of extracting their essence and common sense and incorporating it as your own, to give your physical existence meaning.

Now, during the second stage or phase of the impregnation of this religious doctrine, you began to acquire survival skills, and you were thus reclassified as "The Walking Dead." Although, still in your dazed catatonic state, some of you who were fortunate enough to have consumed a multitude of brain matter became leaders and preachers and began to propagate and formulate a plan to mobilize and unite the masses of the walking dead to eradicate all of those who were not of them and to bring them under subjection. There go your religious zealots and fanatics. So, they all embarked upon such a campaign, and all of those bitten were being transformed into one of the walking dead. You were ultimately circumvented and restrained.

And while you were in this restrictive environmental condition, and the third and final stage or phase of your impregnation, those of you who had risen to the level of leadership roles came into a mutual form of agreement with society, to do society's bidding and that society would aid them in their escape from confinement. All of this occurred without the walking dead not realizing or knowing that this small group of people were in actuality their original creators, So they schemed and orchestrated what can be termed a successful prison break; and again, you were ultimate reclassified as "The Return of the Living Dead," as you have displayed the propensity to be very lethal and dangerous.

And since your return, you have been doing society's bidding; even though society has been placing many of you in their prisons, you have caused and have been doing nothing short of destroying the social fabric of the world and defacing nature with your jargon, in comport with your psychological programming, and as zealots and fanatics in the name(s) of your respective religions, and in the name of a God – which is not a name at all, for it is only a title of nobility and an acronym… that you have never seen, nor have you been able to envision or identify yourselves within an attempt at entering into what is termed "The Pearly Gates" – Kingdom of Heaven.

"Enter ye in at the strait gate: for wide is the gate, and broad is the way, that leadeth to destruction, and many there be which go in thereat: Because strait is the gate, and narrow is the way, which leadeth unto life, and few there be that find it. Matt. 7:13-14

It is self–evident that the Sacred Books are circulated everywhere on Earth, and they serve as the basis for the many different religious factions. Moreover, and notwithstanding, that for who among you that understands the arcane meanings and concepts contained within what is termed religious books? And who amongst you has complete conscious awareness of what is transcribed in each verse? For you, the masses have limited themselves to either just to believe or too flat-out reject or deny it. Such people have developed a very highly specialized and sophisticated psychological idiosyncrasy of a different and fatal type of logical system.

You, the masses of the people, are without a purpose and meaning, substance, or value, and therefore your lives appear to be dark and gloomy, for you possess no light within; so, you are resigned to just living to die. And this does not have to be so.

Hear Me all of those who have ears to hear and see Me all of you who have eyes to see… and know **THAT I AM** Extends Greetings of Salutation by Visitation and has sent Me only to convey a message. You must know that all visible objects to Man are only perfunctory walls. But in every event of the act of living, and the undoubtable deed therein lies something unknown, but still, this unreasoning thing that puts forth its hand and the moldings of its features from behind this unreasoning wall.

If only Man would strike with the force of reason, strike through this unreasoning wall. For how will a prisoner be able to reach outside and free himself from his mental state of bondage except by thrusting through this damnable wall? To Me, religion and this language called jargon is this unreasonable and damnable wall that has been imposed upon the masses of the people. It exudes the impression that there is nothing in existence beyond it. I perceive outrageous strength, with inscrutable malice and malicious intent – the agent-principal of mental and spiritual psychological destruction. I Am being tasked, and with the aid of the Divine Creator – The Grand Architect of the Universe, I will prevail. I Self Lord Am Master!

Chapter Four

Philosophy

In our quest to comprehend the unknown, a method of discernment was formulated and established that would, to a degree, would facilitate and aid our efforts for understanding the Divine creation of the cosmos. It has been classified as a philosophy in today's terminology. You may pose the question: What is the meaning of philosophy? Society, as we know it, has catalogized philosophy as a childish superstitious attempt and concealment of our ignorance of the unknown; but, when it is impressed upon Society, thus to provide us with an explanation of the Divine creation, it is sans a practical response, and simply utter that it is not for us to know. So, to answer: Philosophy, as I know it and wish to convey, is a study of the law of cause and effect and its relation to things and ideas; serene wisdom emanating from a calm contemplation of life and our material universe.

Philosophy can also be described as a dogma. In the Greek language, philosophy is described as Dogma – a theological doctrine of the Divine Universe. The Greek word from whence dogma had its origin has, as its meaning, to think. Dogma thus means the apprehension of the rationale and meaning of things

The term God also has its origin in and derived from the Greek language. It is also an acronym depicting and characterizing an individual Being of Supreme Intelligence, Wisdom, and Power. The word God translated is Gomar Oz Dumar and means Strength, Wisdom, and Beauty. This was the nature in which the Greeks viewed and described the character of this Great Being, who had come to liberate them from a mental state of darkness to a living perpendicular.

I Am not conveying the term philosophy from a conventional standpoint or point of view, but what I mean by way of philosophy derives from My knowledge and comprehension of the teachings, as provided by The Most Honorable Elijah Muhammad, and under the banner of The Honorable Minister Louis Farrakhan, who was raised among us as a people, who was a mentally dead and sad people, to restore us to life. His teachings and lessons are a life-supplying source. A well of water for the dry bones. His philosophical teaching of the Divine Creator provides arcane meanings and concepts designed to stimulate the mind.

The teaching on the surface appears to be conventional in some respects, but in essence, upon reflection, contains a profound and deeper hidden message, that from a glance, it will escape the prying eyes of the profane; what the teachings are concerned with is the strengthening of the mind. Something the profane just simply does not care to partake in.

The teachings of The Most Honorable Elijah Muhammad transcend the token of time as it is commonly known, in its conventional form. The teachings convey that time does not exist in the higher realms. The teachings are profound and provocative. And upon reflection, I perceive that there is no time in eternity; it does not exist, as it does not maintain a basic, concrete, objective, or exact authentic and legitimate origin.

The advent of time appeared during our early stages of mental growth and development in the contemplation of our material universe, based upon the cosmic phenomena occurring today within the eternal movements in our universe. As it has turned out, many successive phenomena exist in our universe. For it is self–evident that when the different successive phenomena occurring in our universe start to formulate and crystalize – manifest themselves on the physical realm, the advent of time comes to the forefront. In rapid succession, the creation of the Sun, the Moon, and the Stars are phenomena governed by laws. Philosophy can be viewed upon under many different lights and by many different people from all walks of life. Philosophy is subjective and distinguishes human characteristics, as defined by human behavior, exteriorized by our thought activity.

Nothing in our material universe does originate from the human mind. Wherefore, there exists no creature or animal that does not bear the imprint signature of human psychological behavior, i.e., pigs, birds, dogs, horses, mules, donkeys, monkeys, vultures, buzzards, apes, worms, maggots, flies, frogs, butterflies, serpents, reptiles, sheep, wolves, chickens, bugs, hyenas, roaches, rodents, and all the creatures of the seas, oceans, lakes, ponds, and rivers, just to name a few, all bear the essence and nature of a human subject. Just look around, reflect and bear witness to this fact. This is philosophy, the comprehension of Man`s interrelation with the manifested objects in this material universe.

The concept of philosophy extends to the religious text, our understanding of the Divine Creator, and the message He wishes to convey to His royal subjects in many aspects. In Genesis chapter two, Adam was given the task of naming the animals, i.e., classifying them, for to name means defining and classifying their natures. The naming means understanding the creator`s creative order of things in our material universe.

The distinguishing in the difference between Heaven and Hell as contained within the religious text, and do they exist as a place in which we have to die to reach and experience such places. And the realization of where this Heaven and Hell reside and how we get to them. But upon My constant reflection, I discovered that Heaven and Hell were not someplace that I had to die to achieve, for Heaven and Hell, in all actuality, are states and conditions of the mind. For one cannot really or truly experience neither this Heavenly-like state nor the Hell-like state dead because physical death of the body is complete termination. These are conditions manifested by the mind that the physical and mental stimulation must experience.

The religious texts are rife with philosophical implications for the curious and reflective mind, i.e., Adam and Eve, Tree of Good and Evil, Tree of Life, the Serpent, and the Dragon. The allegory of the Dragon, as found in Revelation, and its explanation derived from philosophy, as someone(s) desire to comprehend its nature and physical existence and its relationship to Man.

It also can be found stationed in the great halls of the Great British Museum, depicting an image representing the Tree of Good and Evil, as found in Genesis two, the apparent apple tree of Eden. And they're close to this tree, there appears two human figures, a man and a woman, depicting Adam and Eve of the Garden, sitting on each side of this tree and reaching up to this tree with the explicit purpose of partaking of its fruit and devouring them; and at the back of this tree lies the dragon serpent, and above the tree is a patch of clouds containing beings, which appear to be looking down and cursing the tree.

"And the Lord God commanded the man, saying, of every tree of the garden thou mayest freely eat; but of the tree of the knowledge of good and evil, thou shalt not eat of it." Gen. 2:16-17

I surmise and take these beings in the clouds as those residing in their assumed loftiness as religious leaders over the masses of the people; carrying their multitude of religious books and doctrine, and not comprehending that which is in their possession, and out of ignorance in an attempt to gain and maintain control of the masses of the people, as they have falsified and changed that which they did not and do not understand so, as you can see that they have deliberately set out to deceive and mislead the masses to their just ends.

My objective here is to convey and project to you the draught of a systematization of such considerable depth in the lack of one`s ability to understand the Divine Creator. Now, you have received, not the spirit of this world, but that spirit in which is of the Creator; so that you might come to know and understand the things that have been freely given to you by the Creator. I also speak of things that are not in words taught by the wisdom of your religious leaders, but that which the Divine Creator teaches, comparing spiritual things with the spiritual. But the carnal man does not receive the things of the Spirit of the Creator; for they are foolishness unto him; neither can he know them, because they are of spiritual discernment. But he that is spiritual judges all things, yet no man judges him himself. For who has known the Creator's mind, that he may instruct him? But we will have the mind of the Cosmic Christ.

Chapter Five

Born Again

We have reached a crossroad, and the condition of our mental state will determine the path we will travel. At some time or another, we have heard what is commonly termed and known in the Christian world, and religious doctrine is "Born Again." And the follower of this doctrine assures the rest of the world that they have been Born Again in their Lord and Savior Jesus Christ. Many of us distinguish this very profound statement of being born again without fully grasping or comprehending the totality of their declaration. For how is it really and truly possible to be born again, and at the same time remain living the same type of life and acting out the same activities before being born again and sometimes worse than before. Something in this milk is not clean. It is contaminated – impure!

"Verily, verily, I say unto thee, Except a man be born again, he cannot see the kingdom of God. "John 3:3

When one is born again, they have been transformed into a new and different and better individual than they once appeared to be. All of their negative vices and inclinations dissipate and are no longer of any interest to them anymore. To be born again (a rebirth) means to revive; resurrect; resuscitate; restore to a former high standing or stature; the re-emergence into existence; acting as a prime directive in a transformation.

To be born again means to enter into the Creator's Marvelous Light and be transformed, and therefore become a reflection of the Light of the Grand Architect of the Universe, for you have become one with the Creator, reflecting His Glory. Your thoughts, activities, actions in dealing with others, and you reflect the Creator's thoughts, His actions, and His exercising righteous judgment.

"Verily, verily, I say unto thee, Except a man be born of water and the Spirit, he cannot enter into the kingdom of God. That which is born of the flesh is flesh, and that which is born of the Spirit is spirit. Marvel not that I said unto thee, Ye must be born again." John 3:5-7

To be born again, one must transcend the conventional system and its modes of operation(s) and rise to a new and improved level in the mental state of consciousness into self–realization. Here is an age-old Riddle of the Ancients: With no wings, I fly, with no arms I climb, with no eyes I see, I Am more frightening than any beast; stronger than any foe, I Am cunning, ruthless and tall, in the end, I rule all. What Am I? Contemplate this very profound affirmation and reflect upon its meaning.

To truly be born again means that we must conquer and overcome our animalistic desires and transform ourselves into the Consciousness of the Grand Architect of the Universe, thus becoming manifestations of His Light. Only by awakening, the consciousness will one truly see the straight, narrow, and most difficult path leading to the Marvelous Light.

The Creator is the Light of the Heavens and the Earth. The parable of His Light is as if there were a niche and within it, a lamp enclosed in glass; the glass, as it were a brilliant star, lit from a blessed tree, an olive, neither of the East nor of the West, whose oil is well-nigh luminous, though fire scarce touched it; Light upon Light, the Creator guides whom He will to His Light.

A niche is a recess, an area secure and accessible from one direction; the lamp is the accumulation of wealth of knowledge, radiating from within – The Mind; glass is a sphere or orb that contains energy, a substance of value and its manifestation of the Mind; the tree is the physical body – the machine, upon which the sphere or orb resides; as the mind controls the mechanical functions of the body.

The physical body is endowed with five faculties of perception: (1) the faculty of sensory, which collects all the information accrued by the senses; (2) the imaginative faculty, which transcribes the information conveyed by the senses and then transmits it to the Intellectual faculty when it is required; (3) the Intellectual faculty, thus apprehends the ideas beyond the sphere of the sense and imagination; as these ideas are universal in their application, symbolizing the particular things that are known by the senses; (4) the ratiocinative faculty, operating in the realm of reason, takes the information and combines them and deduces an abstract knowledge;(5) the faculty of transcendental enlightenment, which processes the information into a code of conduct in the material manifestation into how Man should and is too govern Him Self.

To be born again, one must be ready and willing to sacrifice oneself at the altar of the Divine Creator and enter into the cave – the sanctum sanctorium and receive instructions in the Oracles of the Eternal Light and enter into the Kingdom of Heaven.

We must come into a self–realization of ourselves and our relation to the Divine Creator, and be born again into His Marvelous Light, to when the two converge and are joined together, then and only then will we be able to proclaim that I and the Father – who art in Heaven are One. Self-realization is the realization of the Divine and the true nature of the self.

"Who has measured the waters in the hollow of his hand, meted out heaven with the span, comprehended the dust of the earth in a measure, and weighed the mountains in scales and the hills in a balance?" Isa. 40:12

There exists an invisible world, with a light all of its own, and it is very much, quite different from this visible world in which we know, as it also possesses its physical light. The former realm is the Spiritual World, far above this physical world. This Spiritual World is not in space as we have been commonly taught it to be, for there is no distinction of space, only grades and degrees of ascension.

Behold, I show you a mystery; we shall not all sleep, but we shall all be changed. This corruption must put on incorruption, and this mortal must put on immortality. So, when this corruptible shall have put on incorruption, and this mortal shall have put on immortality, the written saying shall be brought to pass. Death has now been swallowed up in victory.

So, when one is born again, they have ascended and been transformed into a different person and will ultimately be moved into the Hereafter". Who can explain what the hereafter is? The Hereafter implies the out with the old and in with the new and improved body and mind, destroying negative vices and inclinations while building positive virtues and moral character. Supreme Mathematics!

References

Technology ("science of craft", from Greek τέχνη, techne, "art, skill, cunning of hand"; and -λογία, - logia) is the sum of any techniques, skills, methods, and processes used in the production of goods or services or in the accomplishment of objectives, such as scientific investigation. Technology can be the knowledge of techniques, processes, and the like, or it can be embedded in machines to allow for operation without detailed knowledge of their workings. Systems (e.g., machines) applying technology by taking an input, changing it according to the system's use, and then producing an outcome are referred to as technology systems or technological systems.

The simplest form of technology is the development and use of basic tools. The prehistoric invention of shaped stone tools followed by the discovery of how to control fire increased sources of food. The later Neolithic Revolution extended this and quadrupled the sustenance available from a territory. The invention of the wheel helped humans to travel in and control their environment.

Developments in historic times, including the printing press, the telephone, and the Internet, have lessened physical barriers to communication and allowed humans to interact freely on a global scale.

Technology has many effects. It has helped develop more advanced economies (including today's global economy) and has allowed the rise of a leisure class. Many technological processes produce unwanted by-products known as pollution and deplete natural resources to the detriment of Earth's environment. Innovations have always influenced the values of a society and raised new questions in the ethics of technology. Examples include the rise of the notion of efficiency in terms of human productivity, and the challenges of bioethics.

Philosophical debates have arisen over the use of technology, with disagreements over whether technology improves the human condition or worsens it. Neo-Luddism, anarcho-primitivism, and similar reactionary movements criticize the pervasiveness of technology, arguing that it harms the environment and alienates people; proponents of ideologies such as transhumanism and techno progressivism view continued technological progress as beneficial to society and the human condition The use of the term "technology" has changed significantly over the last 200 years. Before the 20th century, the term was uncommon in English, and it was used either to refer to the description or study of the useful arts or to allude to technical education, as in the Massachusetts Institute of

Technology (chartered in 1861). The term "technology" rose to prominence in the 20th century in connection with the Second

Industrial Revolution. The term's meanings changed in the early 20th century when

American social scientists, beginning with Thorstein Veblen, translated ideas from the German concept of Technik into "technology." In German and other European languages, a distinction exists between technik and technologie that is absent in English, which usually translates both terms as "technology." By the 1930s, "technology" referred not only to the study of the industrial arts but to the industrial arts themselves.

In 1937, the American sociologist Read Bain wrote that "technology includes all tools, machines, utensils, weapons, instruments, housing, clothing, communicating and transporting devices and the skills by which we produce and use them." Bain's definition remains common among scholars today, especially social scientists. Scientists and engineers usually prefer to define technology using dictionary definitions; Dictionaries and scholars have offered a variety of definitions. The Merriam-Webster Learner's Dictionary offers a definition of the term: "the use of science in industry, engineering, etc., to invent useful things or to solve problems" and "a machine, piece of equipment, method, etc., that is created by technology."[8] Ursula Franklin, in her 1989 "Real World of Technology" lecture, gave another definition of the concept; it is "practice, the way we do things around here." The term is often used to imply a specific field of technology, or to refer to high technology or just consumer electronics, rather than technology. Bernard Stiegler, in Technics and Time, 1, defines technology in two ways: as "the pursuit of life by means other than life," and as "organized inorganic matter."

Publisher: Wikipedia, The Free Encyclopedia. Permanent link: https://en.wikipedia.org/w/index.php?title=Technology&oldid=1065929615

TRICKNOLOGY

In the beliefs of the Nation of Islam (NOI), Yakub (sometimes spelled *Yacub or Yaqub*) was a black scientist who lived 6,600 years ago and began the creation of the white race/whites. He is said to have done this through a form of selective breeding which is referred to as "grafting", while he was living on the island of Patmos. The Nation of Islam's theology states that Yakub is the biblical Jacob. The story has caused disputes within the NOI during its history. Under its current leader Louis Farrakhan, the NOI continues to assert that the story of Yakub is true, claiming that modern science is consistent with it.

The story of Yakub originated in the writings of Wallace Fard Muhammad, the founder of the Nation of Islam, in his doctrinal Q&A pamphlet Lost Found Moslem Lesson No. 2. It was developed by his successor Elijah Muhammad in several writings, most fully in a chapter entitled

"The Making of Devil" in his book Message to the Blackman in America.

Yakub is said to have been born in Mecca at a time when 30% of original black people were "dissatisfied". He was a member of the Meccan branch of the Tribe of Shabazz. Yakub acquired the nickname "big head", because of his unusually large head and his arrogance. At the age of six, he discovered the law of attraction and repulsion by playing with magnets made of steel.

This insight led to a plan to create new people. He "saw an unlike human being, made to attract others, who could, with the knowledge of tricks and lies, rule the original black man." By the age of 18, he had exhausted all knowledge in the universities of Mecca. He then discovered that the original black man contained both a "black germ" and a "brown germ". With 59,999 followers, he went to an "isle in the Aegean Sea called Pelan", which Muhammad identifies with Patmos. Once there, he established a despotic regime and set about breeding out the black traits, killed all darker babies, and created a brown race after 200 years.

Yakub died at the age of 152, but his followers carried on his work. After 600 years of these deliberate eugenics, the white race was created. The brutal conditions of their creation determined the evil nature of the new race: "by lying to the black mother of the baby, this lie was born into the very nature of the white baby; and, murder for the black people was also born in them— or made by nature a liar and murderer".

The new race traveled to Mecca where they caused so much trouble they were exiled to "West Asia (Europe), and stripped of everything but the language....Once there, they were roped in, to keep them out of Paradise....The soldiers patrolled the border armed with swords, to prevent the devils from crossing." For many centuries they lived a barbaric life, surviving naked in caves and eating raw meat, but eventually they were drawn out of the caves by Moses who "taught them to wear clothes". Moses tried to civilize them, but eventually gave up and blew up 300 of the most troublesome of them with dynamite.

However, they had learned to use "tricknology" a plan to use their lack of empathy, emotion, and trickery to usurp power and enslave the black population, bringing the first slaves to America. The plan was carried out using the Yakubian's "sidemouth", according to the myth Yakubian's lack all emotional intelligence and exist as unfeeling, unnaturally created predators. According to The Autobiography of Malcolm X, all the races other than the black race were by-products of Yakub's (spelled Yacub in the biography) work, as the "red, yellow and brown" races were created during the "bleaching" process; however, the "black race" included Asian peoples, considered to be shared ancestors of the Moors.

"Whites" were defined as Europeans. Elijah Muhammad also asserted that some of the new white race "tried to graft themselves back into

the black nation, but they had nothing to go by."
As a result, they became gorillas. "A few were
lucky enough to make a start and got as far as
what you call the gorilla. In fact, all of the mon-
key family are from this 2,000-year history of
the white race in Europe."

According to NOI doctrine, Yakub's progeny
were destined to rule for 6,000 years before the
original black peoples of the world regained
dominance, a process that had begun in 1914.

Yakub and Jacob

The name Ya`qub (Yakub) is the Arabic var-
iant of the name of the Biblical Patriarch known
as Jacob in English language versions of the Bi-
ble, and as Ya`qob in Biblical Hebrew. Fard Mu-
hammad's Yakub has some parallels to the Biblical Jacob's role as the father of the tribes of Is-
rael. The idea that Jews were an "artificial race"
created by interbreeding and dependent on
"tricks and lies" already existed in anti-Semitic
theories of the time. The story of Yakub includes

Jews as part of a wider artificially created "white" race.

The NOI's claim that Jacob altered the skin color of a specific group of humans through selective breeding is similar to a story in Genesis 30:37–43 where Jacob alters the fur color of the goats and sheep in his uncle Laban's flocks. One major difference is that while the NOI says that Yakub employed selective breeding, Jacob used sympathetic magic in the Old Testament story.

In speeches by Malcolm X, Yakub is identified completely with Jacob. Referring to the story of Jacob wrestling with the angel, Malcolm X states that Elijah Muhammad told him that "Jacob was Yacub, and the angel that Jacob wrestled with wasn't God, it was the government of the day". This was because Yakub was seeking funds for his expedition to Patmos, "so when it says Jacob wrestled with an angel, 'angel' is only used as a symbol to hide the one he was really wrestling with". However, Malcolm X also states that John of Patmos was also Yakub, and that the Book of Revelation refers to his deeds: "John was Yacub. John was out there getting ready to make a new race, he said, for the word of the Lord".

Sources

Ernest Allen argues that "the Yakub myth may have been created out of whole cloth by Prophet Fard". Allen says the Yakub story could conceivably have been influenced by a real historical event during the struggle between Muslims and Christians for control of Spain. Muslim leader Abu Yusuf Yaqub al-Mansur defeated the Franks at the Battle of Alarcos (1195). After the battle 40,000 European prisoners of war were taken to Morocco to labor on Yaqub's building projects. They were then set free and "allowed to form a valley settlement located somewhere between Fez and Marrakesh. On his deathbed Ya'qub lamented his decision to allow these Shibanis (as they came to be called) to form an enclave on Moroccan soil, thereby posing a potential threat to the stability of the Moorish empire."

Yusuf Nuruddin says that a more direct source was the doctrine of the "Yacobites" propounded by Timothy Drew's Moorish Science Temple, to which Fard had probably belonged before he founded the NOI. According to Drew, early pre-Columbian civilizations were founded by a West African Moor "named Yakub who landed on the Yucatan peninsula". This derived from the then-current notion that the gigantic heads created by the ancient Olmec peoples of the Yucatán area had "negroid" features (see Olmec alternative origin speculations), which had led Leo Wiener to argue that they were from West Africa.

They [Drew's followers] said that the huge stone heads attested to the fact that the Yakubites evolved into a race of scientific geniuses with large heads (as depicted in the sculptures) and small bodies. This legend of Yakub—a big-headed scientist—finds its way into the mythology of the Nation of Islam, indicating that the founders of the NOI, W. D. Farrad and Elijah Muhammad, were influenced by the Moorish Science Temple, and were possibly even members.

Harold Bloom in his book The American Religion argues that Yakub combines elements of the biblical God and the Gnostic concept of the Demiurge, saying that "Yakub has an irksome memorability as a crude but pungent Gnostic Demiurge". Nathaniel Deutsch also notes that Fard and Muhammad draw on the concept of the Demiurge, along with traditions of esotericism in Biblical interpretation, absorbing aspects of Biblical tales to the new narrative, such as the swords of the Muslim warriors keeping the "white devils" from Paradise, like the flaming sword of the angel protecting the Garden of Eden in Genesis.

Edward Curtis calls the story "a black theodicy: a story grounded in a mythological view of history that explained the fall of black civilization, the Middle Passage from Africa to the Americas, and the practice of Christian religion among slaves and their descendants."

Several commentators state that the story, by associating blacks with ancient high civilizations and whites with cave-dwelling barbarians and gorillas, both uses and spectacularly reverses the populist and scientific racism of the era which identified Africans as primitive, or closer to apes than whites. This drew on earlier criticisms of white supremacist Nordicism, creating a mythic version of "attacks on Anglo-Saxon lineage and behavior that had been voiced by more mainstream black thinkers during the nineteenth century....With these references the [NOI] Muslims replicated the images of European savagery in the Middle Ages that were so pervasive in nineteenth-century black racial thought." Deutsch says that "Muhammad anchored his radical doctrine within the context of an established scriptural tradition" of Biblical exegesis, which "was therefore a sophisticated form of racism against whites."

Role in the Nation of Islam

The doctrine of Yakub was one of the reasons for splits in the Nation of Islam. Malcolm X in his Autobiography notes that, in his travels in the Middle East, many Muslims reacted with shock upon hearing about the doctrine of Yakub, which, while present in NOI theology, does not appear in mainstream Islam. He rejected the story in his later statements, asserting that anyone of any race who intentionally deprives others of basic human rights is a "devil". Warith Deen Mohammed, who took over the Nation of Islam after his father Elijah's death rejected it almost immediately and tried to re-invent the Nation as a mainstream Sunni Islam movement.

Louis Farrakhan reinstated the original Nation of Islam and has reasserted his belief in the literal truth of the story of Yakub. In a 1996 interview, Henry Louis Gates, Chairman of

Harvard University's Afro-American Studies Department, asked him whether the story was a metaphor or literal. Farrakhan claimed that aspects of the story had been proven accurate by modern genetic science and insisted that "Personally, I believe that Yakub is not a mythical figure—he is a very real scientist. Not a big-head silly thing, as they would like to say."

Farrakhan's periodical The Final Call continues to publish articles arguing that modern science supports the accuracy of Elijah Muhammad's account of Yakub. The NOI splinter groups the Five-Percent Nation and the United Nation of Islam also believe in the Yakub doctrine.

Author: Wikipedia contributors. Wikipedia, The Free Encyclopedia. Permanent link: https://en.wikipedia.org/w/index.php?title=Yakub_(Nation_of_Islam)&oldid=1066515408